SO SWEET
to knit

S

If you're looking for c..... ....ꞁⅇ for the newborn, then this heavenly collection is just for you! Mom will go gaga over the **2 knit and 3 crochet wraps** featuring adorable finishing touches like ruffles, ribbons, fringe, and other edgings. Our **clear instructions** and **full-color photographs** help you every step of the way in creating just the right wrap for the New Arrival.

GENERAL INSTRUCTIONS

ABBREVIATIONS

ch(s)	chain(s)
dc	double crochet(s)
K	knit
mm	millimeters
P	purl
P2SSO	pass 2 slipped stitches over
Rnd(s)	Round(s)
sc	single crochet(s)
sp(s)	space(s)
st(s)	stitch(es)
tbl	through back loop(s)
tog	together
YO	yarn over

★ — work instructions following ★ as many **more** times as indicated in addition to the first time.

† to † — work all instructions from first † to second † **as many** times as specified.

( ) or [ ] — work enclosed instructions **as many** times as specified by the number immediately following **or** work all enclosed instructions in the stitch or space indicated **or** contains explanatory remarks.

colon (:) — the number(s) given after a colon at the end of a row or round denote(s) the number of stitches you should have on that row or round.

©1999 by Leisure Arts, Inc.
5701 Ranch Drive, Little Rock, AR 72223   **2**   ISBN 1-57486-995-7

GAUGE

Exact gauge is **essential** for proper size. Hook or needle size given in instructions is merely a guide and should never be used without first making a sample swatch approximately 4" square in the stitch, yarn, and hook or needle specified. Then measure it, counting your stitches and rows or rounds carefully. If your swatch is larger or smaller than specified, **make another, changing hook or needle size to get the correct gauge.** Keep trying until you find the size hook that will give you the specified gauge.

CROCHET BASICS
POST STITCH

Work around post of stitch indicated, inserting hook in direction of arrow *(Fig. 1)*.

Fig. 1

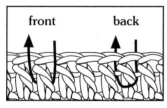

front   back

FREE LOOPS OF A CHAIN

When instructed to work in free loops of a chain, work in loop indicated by arrow *(Fig. 2)*.

Fig. 2

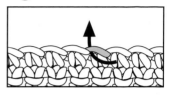

KNIT BASICS
PURL THROUGH THE BACK LOOP

With yarn in front, insert the right needle into the **back** of the next stitch from **back** to **front** *(Fig. 3)* and purl it.

Fig. 3

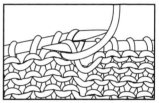

YARN OVER
(abbreviated YO)

Bring the yarn **forward** between the needles, then back **over** the top of the right hand needle, so that it is now in position to knit the next stitch *(Fig. 4)*.

Fig. 4

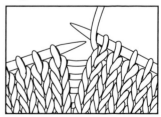

KNIT 2 TOGETHER

(abbreviated K2 tog)
Insert the right needle into the **front** of the first two stitches on the left needle as if to **knit** *(Fig. 5)*, then **knit** them together.

Fig. 5

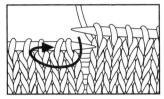

KNIT 2 TOGETHER THROUGH THE BACK LOOPS

(abbreviated K2 tog tbl)
Insert the right needle into the **back** of the first two stitches on the left needle from **front** to **back** *(Fig. 6)* and knit them together.

Fig. 6

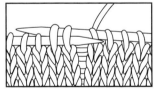

SLIP 2, KNIT 1, PASS 2 SLIPPED STITCHES OVER

(abbreviated slip 2, K1, P2SSO)
With yarn in back, separately slip two stitches as if to **knit** *(Fig. 7a)*, then knit the next stitch. With the left needle, bring the two slipped stitches over the knit stitch *(Fig. 7b)* and off the needle.

Fig. 7a

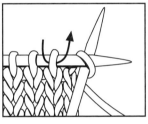

Fig. 7b

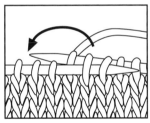

1. RIBBONS & RUFFLES
to crochet

Shown on page 1.

Finished Size:
37" x 48"

MATERIALS
Sport Weight Yarn: 14 ounces, (400 grams, 1,400 yards)
Crochet hook, size G (4.00 mm) **or** size needed for gauge
½"w Ribbon - 7½ yards

GAUGE: In pattern, one repeat = 3¼"; 8 rows = 3"

AFGHAN BODY
Ch 146 **loosely**.

Row 1: Sc in second ch from hook, ★ ch 3, skip next 2 chs, sc in next ch; repeat from ★ across: 49 sc and 48 ch-3 sps.

Row 2 (Right side)**:** Ch 4 **(counts as first dc plus ch 1, now and throughout)**, turn; sc in next ch-3 sp, ch 1, 5 dc in next ch-3 sp, ch 1, sc in next ch-3 sp, ★ (ch 3, sc in next ch-3 sp) 3 times, ch 1, 5 dc in next ch-3 sp, ch 1, sc in next ch-3 sp; repeat from ★ across to last sc, ch 1, dc in last sc: 90 sts and 49 sps.

Row 3: Ch 1, turn; sc in first dc, ch 3, skip next 2 ch-1 sps and next dc, sc in next dc, ch 3, skip next dc, sc in next dc, ch 3, ★ skip next ch-1 sp, sc in next ch-3 sp, ch 1, (dc, ch 1) 3 times in next ch-3 sp, sc in next ch-3 sp, ch 3, skip next ch-1 sp and next dc, sc in next dc, ch 3, skip next dc, sc in next dc, ch 3; repeat from ★ across to last 2 ch-1 sps, skip last 2 ch-1 sps, sc in last dc: 67 sts and 66 sps.

Row 4: Ch 4, turn; sc in next ch-3 sp, ch 1, 5 dc in next ch-3 sp, ch 1, sc in next ch-3 sp, ★ ch 3, skip next ch-1 sp, (sc in next ch-1 sp, ch 3) twice, skip next ch-1 sp, sc in next ch-3 sp, ch 1, 5 dc in next ch-3 sp, ch 1, sc in next ch-3 sp; repeat from ★ across to last sc, ch 1, dc in last sc: 90 sts and 49 sps.

Rows 5-114: Repeat Rows 3 and 4, 55 times.

Row 115: Ch 5 (counts as first dc plus ch 2), turn; skip next sc, dc in next dc, ch 2, skip next 3 dc, dc in next dc, ch 2, ★ skip next ch-1 sp, dc in next ch-3 sp, ch 2, sc in next ch-3 sp, ch 2, dc in next ch-3 sp, ch 2, skip next sc, dc in next dc, ch 2, skip next 3 dc, dc in next dc, ch 2; repeat from ★ across to last 2 ch-1 sps, skip last 2 ch-1 sps, dc in last dc; do **not** finish off: 49 sts and 48 ch-2 sps.

EDGING

Rnd 1: Ch 1, turn; working in sts and chs across Row 115, sc in first dc, ch 1, (skip next st, sc in next st, ch 1) across to last 2 sts, skip next ch, (sc, ch 2, sc) in last dc, ch 1; working in end of rows, sc in first row, ch 1, sc in next row, ch 1, skip next row, [(sc in next row, ch 1) 3 times, skip next row] across; working in free loops of beginning ch **(Fig. 2, page 3)**, (sc, ch 2, sc) in ch at base of first sc, ch 1, (skip next ch, sc in next ch, ch 1) across to last 2 chs, skip next ch, (sc, ch 2, sc) in last ch, ch 1; working in end of rows, skip first row, (sc in next row, ch 1) 3 times, [skip next row, (sc in next row, ch 1) 3 times] across to last 3 rows, skip next row, (sc in next row, ch 1) twice, sc in same st as first sc, ch 2; join with slip st to first sc: 322 sc.

Rnd 2: Ch 1, do **not** turn; sc in same st, (ch 1, sc in next sc) across to next corner ch-2 sp, (sc, ch 2, sc) in corner ch-2 sp, ★ sc in next sc, (ch 1, sc in next sc) across to next corner ch-2 sp, (sc, ch 2, sc) in corner ch-2 sp; repeat from ★ 2 times **more**; join with slip st to first sc: 330 sc and 322 sps.

Rnd 3 (Eyelet rnd)**:** Slip st in first ch-1 sp, ch 4, ★ (dc in next ch-1 sp, ch 1) across to within 2 sc of next corner ch-2 sp, skip next sc, dc in next sc, (dc, ch 3, dc) in corner ch-2 sp, dc in next sc, ch 1; repeat from ★ around; join with slip st to first dc.

Rnd 4: Ch 4, dc in same st, ch 1, dc in next dc, ch 1, ★ [(dc, ch 1) twice in next dc, dc in next dc, ch 1] across to next corner ch-3 sp, (dc, ch 1) 5 times in corner ch-3 sp, skip next dc, dc in next dc, ch 1, [(dc, ch 1) twice in next dc, dc in next dc, ch 1] across to within one dc of next corner ch-3 sp, skip next dc, (dc, ch 1) 5 times in corner ch-3 sp, skip next dc, dc in next dc, ch 1; repeat from ★ once **more**; join with slip st to first dc.

Rnd 5: Ch 1, sc in same st, ch 1, sc in next dc, ch 1, (dc, ch 1) twice in next dc, ★ (sc in next dc, ch 1) twice, (dc, ch 1) twice in next dc; repeat from ★ around; join with slip st to first sc.

Rnd 6: Slip st in first ch-1 sp, ch 1, sc in same sp, ch 1, skip next sc, dc in next dc, ch 1, (dc, ch 1) twice in next ch-1 sp, dc in next dc, ch 1, skip next ch-1 sp, ★ sc in next ch-1 sp, ch 1, skip next sc, dc in next dc, ch 1, (dc, ch 1) twice in next ch-1 sp, dc in next dc, ch 1, skip next ch-1 sp; repeat from ★ around; join with slip st to first sc, finish off.

Working across **length** of Afghan, weave a 72" length of ribbon through Eyelet rnd; repeat across opposite side.

Working across **width** of Afghan, weave a 63" length of ribbon through Eyelet rnd; repeat across opposite side.

Tie ribbons in a bow at each corner and trim as desired.

Design by Anne Halliday.

---

2. HEARTWARMING WRAP
to crochet
Shown on Front Cover.

Finished Size:
33" x 43"

MATERIALS
Sport Weight Yarn: 17 ounces, (480 grams, 1,715 yards)
Crochet hook, size F (3.75 mm) **or** size needed for gauge
½" Ribbon - 6 yards

GAUGE: In pattern,
16 dc = 4"; 10 rows = 4¼"

AFGHAN BODY
Ch 107 **loosely**.

Row 1 (Eyelet row)**:** Dc in eighth ch from hook, ★ ch 2, skip next 2 chs, dc in next ch; repeat from ★ across: 34 sps.

Row 2: Ch 5 **(counts as first dc plus ch 2, now and throughout)**, turn; dc in next dc, (2 dc in next ch-2 sp, dc in next dc) across to beginning ch, ch 2, skip next 2 chs, dc in next ch: 99 dc.

To work Double Cluster, YO, insert hook from **front** to **back** around post of dc **below** last dc worked *(Fig. 1, page 3)*, † YO and pull up a loop, YO and draw through 2 loops on hook, YO, insert hook from **front** to **back** around **same** dc, YO and pull up a loop, YO and draw through 2 loops on hook †, YO, skip next dc, insert hook from **front** to **back** around post of next dc, repeat from † to † once, YO and draw through all 5 loops on hook.

Row 3 (Right side)**:** Ch 5, turn; dc in next 2 dc, work Double Cluster, ★ dc in same dc and in next 2 dc, work Double Cluster; repeat from ★ across to last 2 dc, dc in same dc and in next dc, ch 2, dc in last dc: 24 Double Clusters.

Row 4: Ch 5, turn; dc in next 2 dc, dc in each Double Cluster and in each dc across to last dc, ch 2, dc in last dc: 99 dc.

Rows 5-83: Repeat Rows 3 and 4, 39 times; then repeat Row 3 once **more**.

Row 84 (Eyelet row)**:** Ch 5, turn; dc in next dc, ch 2, ★ skip next 2 sts, dc in next st, ch 2; repeat from ★ across to last dc, dc in last dc; do **not** finish off: 34 sps.

EDGING

Rnd 1: Ch 1, turn; (sc, ch 5) 3 times in first corner sp, † (sc, ch 5) twice in each sp across to next corner sp, (sc, ch 5) 6 times in corner sp, (sc, ch 5) twice in next sp, (sc in next sp, ch 5) across to next corner sp †, (sc, ch 5) 6 times in corner sp, repeat from † to † once, sc in first corner sp, (ch 5, sc in same sp) twice, ch 2, dc in first sc to form last ch-5 sp: 318 ch-5 sps.

Rnd 2: Ch 1, sc in same sp, (ch 5, sc in next ch-5 sp) around, ch 2, dc in first sc to form last ch-5 sp.

To work Puff St, ★ YO, insert hook in sp indicated, YO and pull up a loop even with loop on hook; repeat from ★ 3 times **more**, YO and draw through all 9 loops on hook.

Rnd 3: Ch 1, sc in same sp, ch 5, sc in next ch-5 sp, ch 5, work Puff St in next ch-5 sp, ★ ch 5, (sc in next ch-5 sp, ch 5) twice, work Puff St in next ch-5 sp; repeat from ★ around, ch 2, dc in first sc to form last ch-5 sp: 106 Puff Sts.

Rnd 4: Ch 1, sc in same sp, ch 5, work Puff St in next ch-5 sp, ch 5, ★ (sc in next ch-5 sp, ch 5) twice, work Puff St in next ch-5 sp, ch 5; repeat from ★ around to last ch-5 sp, sc in last ch-5 sp, ch 2, dc in first sc to form last ch-5 sp.

Rnd 5: Ch 1, work Puff St in same sp, (ch 5, sc in next ch-5 sp) twice, ★ ch 5, work Puff St in next ch-5 sp, (ch 5, sc in next ch-5 sp) twice; repeat from ★ around, ch 2, dc in top of first Puff St to form last ch-5 sp.

Rnds 6 and 7: Repeat Rnds 3 and 4.

Rnd 8: Ch 1, sc in same sp, ch 5, sc in third ch from hook, ch 2, ★ sc in next ch-5 sp, ch 5, sc in third ch from hook, ch 2; repeat from ★ around; join with slip st to first sc, finish off.

Weave ribbon through each Eyelet row, leaving a 10" length at each end. Weave ribbon through ch-2 sps on remaining two sides, leaving a 10" length at each end. Tie ends in a bow at each corner.

Design by Terry Kimbrough.

---

3. AIRY DREAM
to crochet
Shown on Back Cover.

Finished Size:
35" x 44"

MATERIALS
Sport Weight Yarn: 15 ounces, (430 grams, 1,420 yards)
Crochet hook, size F (3.75 mm) **or** size needed for gauge

GAUGE: 17 dc and 9 rows = 4"

AFGHAN BODY
Ch 220 **loosely.**

Row 1 (Right side)**:** 2 Dc in fourth ch from hook **(3 skipped chs count as first dc)**, skip next 2 chs, sc in next ch, ch 5, skip next 5 chs, sc in next ch, ★ skip next 2 chs, 5 dc in next ch, skip next 2 chs, sc in next ch, ch 5, skip next 5 chs, sc in next ch; repeat from ★ across to last 3 chs, skip next 2 chs, 3 dc in last ch: 127 sts and 18 ch-5 sps.

Row 2: Ch 1, turn; sc in first dc, ★ ch 5, sc in next ch-5 sp, ch 5, skip next 3 sts, sc in next dc; repeat from ★ across: 37 sc and 36 ch-5 sps.

Row 3: Ch 5 **(counts as first dc plus ch 2)**, turn; sc in first ch-5 sp, 5 dc in next sc, sc in next ch-5 sp, ★ ch 5, sc in next ch-5 sp, 5 dc in next sc, sc in next ch-5 sp; repeat from ★ across to last sc, ch 2, dc in last sc: 128 sts and 19 sps.

Row 4: Ch 1, turn; sc in first dc, ch 5, skip next ch-2 sp and next 3 sts, sc in next dc, ch 5, ★ sc in next ch-5 sp, ch 5, skip next 3 sts, sc in next dc, ch 5; repeat from ★ across to last ch-2 sp, skip last ch-2 sp, sc in last dc: 37 sc and 36 ch-5 sps.

Row 5: Ch 3 **(counts as first dc)**, turn; 2 dc in same st, sc in next ch-5 sp, ch 5, sc in next ch-5 sp, ★ 5 dc in next sc, sc in next ch-5 sp, ch 5, sc in next ch-5 sp; repeat from ★ across to last sc, 3 dc in last sc: 127 sts and 18 ch-5 sps.

Repeat Rows 2-5 for pattern until Afghan measures approximately 43" from beginning ch, ending by working Row 5.

Do **not** finish off.

EDGING

Rnd 1: Ch 1, do **not** turn; work 180 sc evenly spaced across end of rows; working in free loops of beginning ch **(Fig. 2, page 3)**, 3 sc in first ch, work 132 sc evenly spaced across to ch at base of last dc, 3 sc in ch at base of last dc; work 180 sc evenly spaced across end of rows; working across sts on last row, 3 sc in first dc, work 132 sc evenly spaced across to last dc, 3 sc in last dc; join with slip st to first sc: 636 sc.

Rnd 2: Slip st in next sc, ch 1, (sc, ch 3, sc) in same st, skip next 2 sc, ★ (sc, ch 3, sc) in next sc, skip next 2 sc; repeat from ★ around; join with slip st to first sc: 212 ch-3 sps.

To work Picot, ch 3, slip st in top of last sc made.

Rnd 3: Slip st in first ch-3 sp, ch 1, (2 sc, work Picot, 2 sc) in same sp and in each of next 59 ch-3 sps, (3 sc, work Picot, 3 sc) in next ch-3 sp, (2 sc, work Picot, 2 sc) in each of next 44 ch-3 sps, (3 sc, work Picot, 3 sc) in next ch-3 sp, (2 sc, work Picot, 2 sc) in each of next 60 ch-3 sps, (3 sc, work Picot, 3 sc) in next ch-3 sp, (2 sc, work Picot, 2 sc) in each of next 44 ch-3 sps, (3 sc, work Picot, 3 sc) in last ch-3 sp; join with slip st to first sc, finish off.

Design by Shobha Govindan.

4. SOFT & SWEET
to knit

Shown on page 14.

Finished Size:
37" x 48"

MATERIALS

Double Knitting Weight Yarn:
Yellow - 7½ ounces,
(210 grams, 705 yards)
White - 7½ ounces,
(210 grams, 705 yards)
29" Circular knitting needles,
sizes 13 (9.00 mm) **and**
15 (10.00 mm) **or** sizes needed
for gauge

Note: Afghan is made holding one strand of Yellow and one strand of White together.

GAUGE:

With larger size needles,
in Stockinette Stitch,
11 sts and 14 rows = 4"

AFGHAN

With smaller size needles, cast on 89 sts.

Rows 1-13: K1, (P1, K1) across.

Change to larger size needles.

Rows 14-17: (K1, P1) 4 times, knit across to last 8 sts, (P1, K1) 4 times.

Row 18 (Right side)**:** K1, (P1, K1) 4 times, ★ K2 tog *(Fig. 5, page 4)*, YO *(Fig. 4, page 3)*; repeat from ★ across to last 10 sts, K2, (P1, K1) 4 times.

Row 19: K1, (P1, K1) 4 times, purl across to last 9 sts, K1, (P1, K1) 4 times.

Rows 20-24: (K1, P1) 4 times, knit across to last 8 sts, (P1, K1) 4 times.

Row 25: K1, (P1, K1) 4 times, purl across to last 9 sts, K1, (P1, K1) 4 times.

Row 26: (K1, P1) 4 times, knit across to last 8 sts, (P1, K1) 4 times.

Rows 27-45: Repeat Rows 25 and 26, 9 times; then repeat Row 25 once **more.**

Rows 46-49: (K1, P1) 4 times, knit across to last 8 sts, (P1, K1) 4 times.

Row 50: K1, (P1, K1) 4 times, (K2 tog, YO) across to last 10 sts, K2, (P1, K1) 4 times.

Rows 51-151: Repeat Rows 19-50, 3 times; then repeat Rows 19-23 once **more.**

Change to smaller size needles.

Rows 152-164: K1, (P1, K1) across.

Bind off all sts in pattern.

Design by Evelyn A. Clark.

5. DIAMOND LACE
to knit

Shown on Back Cover.

Finished Size:
32" x 42"

MATERIALS

Sport Weight Yarn: 17 ounces, (480 grams, 1,605 yards)
24" Circular knitting needle, size 6 (4.25 mm) **or** size needed for gauge
Crochet hook (for fringe)

GAUGE: In pattern,
22 sts and 34 rows = 4"

AFGHAN

Cast on 175 sts **loosely**.

Row 1 (Right side)**:** Purl across.

Note: Mark last row as **right** side.

Row 2: Slip 1 as if to **knit**, ★ P1 tbl *(Fig. 3, page 3)*, K1; repeat from ★ across.

Row 3: Slip 1 as if to **purl**, purl across.

Row 4: Slip 1 as if to **knit**, (P1 tbl, K1) across.

Rows 5-10: Repeat Rows 3 and 4, 3 times.

Row 11: Slip 1 as if to **purl**, P5, K1, ★ K2 tog *(Fig. 5, page 4)*, YO *(Fig. 4, page 3)*, K1, YO, K2 tog tbl *(Fig. 6, page 4)*, K1; repeat from ★ across to last 6 sts, P6.

Row 12: Slip 1 as if to **knit**, P1 tbl, (K1, P1 tbl) twice, purl across to last 6 sts, (P1 tbl, K1) 3 times.

Row 13: Slip 1 as if to **purl**, P5, K2 tog, YO, K3, YO, ★ [slip 2, K1, P2SSO *(Figs. 7a & b, page 4)*], YO, K3, YO; repeat from ★ across to last 8 sts, K2 tog tbl, P6.

Row 14: Slip 1 as if to **knit**, P1 tbl, (K1, P1 tbl) twice, purl across to last 6 sts, (P1 tbl, K1) 3 times.

Row 15: Slip 1 as if to **purl**, P5, K1, ★ YO, K2 tog tbl, K1, K2 tog, YO, K1; repeat from ★ across to last 6 sts, P6.

Row 16: Slip 1 as if to **knit**, P1 tbl, (K1, P1 tbl) twice, purl across to last 6 sts, (P1 tbl, K1) 3 times.

Row 17: Slip 1 as if to **purl**, P5, K2, YO, slip 2, K1, P2SSO, YO, ★ K3, YO, slip 2, K1, P2SSO, YO; repeat from ★ across to last 8 sts, K2, P6.

Row 18: Slip 1 as if to **knit**, P1 tbl, (K1, P1 tbl) twice, purl across to last 6 sts, (P1 tbl, K1) 3 times.

Repeat Rows 11-18 for pattern until Afghan measures approximately 41" from cast on edge, ending by working Row 18.

Last 10 Rows: Repeat Rows 3 and 4, 5 times.

Bind off all sts **loosely** in pattern.

Add fringe across both ends as follows: Cut a piece of cardboard 7" square. Wind the yarn **loosely** and **evenly** around the cardboard until the card is filled, then cut across one end; repeat as needed. Hold 7 strands of yarn together and fold in half. With **wrong** side of Afghan facing and using a crochet hook, draw the folded end up through the first stitch and pull the loose ends through the folded end *(Fig. 8a)*; draw knot up firmly *(Fig. 8b)*. Repeat, working in every fourth stitch. Lay flat on a hard surface and trim ends.

Design by Shobha Govindan.

Fig. 8a

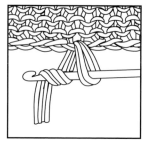

Fig. 8b